THE WINDOW SELLER

THE WINDOW SELLER

Ballari Sen

Paintings by Tamojit Bhattacharya

Published by:

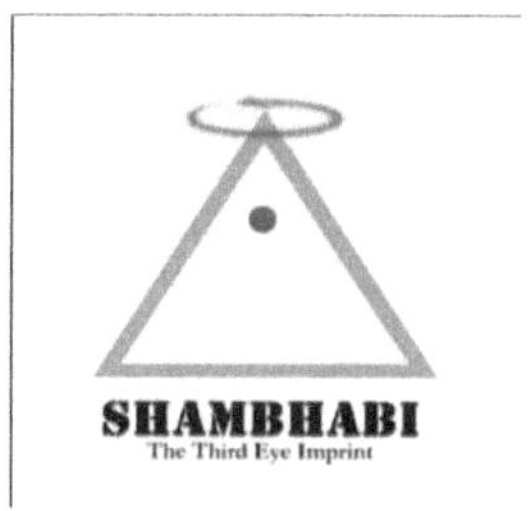

Cover designer: Tamojit Bhattacharya

Price: Rs. One hundred and ninety only (Rs. 190/- only)
U.S. Dollars 9.99 ($9.99)

ISBN: 978-93-83888-14-6

1st Edition: May, 2014.

Published by: **Shambhabi – The Third Eye Imprint**
A-10/1, Amarabati, Sodepur, Calcutta 700110,
India, in association with:

Contact email: kiritisengupta@gmail.com

Printed by (India edition): Cyber Graphics, Calcutta – 36.

Dedicated to

Professor Aditi Lahiri,

Faculty of Linguistics, Philology and Phonetics,

University of Oxford

United Kingdom

Acknowledgements

Heartiest thanks to Tamojit Bhattacharya for his painting titled *The Window Seller*. The title of this wonderful piece of art needs genuine observations on life, its deeper and subtle connotations, especially within our daily introspection where each moment is being sold, distorted and burnt.

Heartfelt thanks to my husband, Dr Aditya Narayan Sen and my son Ayushmaan for being by my side through thick and thin along with all my friends, who have supported and motivated me all through.

Much love and regards to Dr. Kiriti Sengupta, who has been a patient friend all along. His relentless forbearance is highly appreciable.

FOREWORD

Inspirations Mutual

I will define this book as a 'POP Enterprise.' 'POP' denotes Poetry On Painting. The award-winning poet Ballari Sen enters into the domain of Indian English poets through her stunning poetic extravaganza under the title *The Window Seller*. A painting triggered the story! A unique story that changed the course of her life. As a matter of fact the painting shared the same title, and it was done by Tamojit Bhattacharya, a promising artist from Calcutta. Ballari has genuinely acknowledged, "The title of this wonderful piece of art needs genuine observations on life, its deeper and subtle connotations, especially within our daily introspection where each moment is being sold, distorted and burnt." I endorse the notion that poetry delivers only truth! In poetry the 'window' has frequently been used to appreciate fresh inspirations, and here Ballari has admitted the fact in her very first rendition:

"you have grown younger, prettier
may be more inspirational too—'
the windows spoke to me the last Sunday.

blue was his much favorite
so I thought of wearing something...
'something that can't be seen
only the true candid skin will speak..."

Solitude has played its pivotal role in most of her poems that have been included in this thin volume. The poems share some audible hiccups; bumps of the strange mental.

This is evident that the poems have emerged from the silent halo of the poet. Here is an example:

"after miles of unspoken synonyms
as you touched me on my forehead
drenched it with a cologne of gloom
music and mirth, a bell rang away
secret hills and forests and oops!..."

Ballari is indeed a gifted poet; she has even inspired the artist to draw a few paintings based on her poems — *the brothers*, *murshidabad* have been a few of its examples, hence, the phrase, 'inspirations mutual.' *The Window Seller* is essentially a work of art and esthetics; a book that will tease your eyes as well as your psyche - a laudable endeavor!

Kiriti Sengupta*
30th of April, 2014
Calcutta, India.

[*Kiriti Sengupta is a widely published author both in the U.S. and in India. He is the author of the bestselling title *My Glass Of Wine*, a novelette based on autobiographic poetry. He can be reached on www.kiritisengupta.com]

List of Contents

Poems & Paintings	Page number
1. The Window Seller (i – iii)	11-15
2. The Brothers	17
3. Murshidabad	19
4. The Solitary Artist	21
5. Igls: A Thirsty Village	23
6. No	25
7. Tears On The Danube	27
8. The Native	29
9. Stitching Time	31
10. Ash Wednesday	33
11. The Red Planet	35
12. Little Oxford	37
13. Together	39
14. An Age Behind	41
15. The Black And The Red	43
16. The Morning Star	45
17. Snaps	47
18. Madness	49
19. Symphony	51
20. The 'Hello' Window	53
21. Brooding	55
22. The Story Of Three Mugs	57

the window seller

(i)

'you have grown younger, prettier
may be more inspirational too—'
the windows spoke to me the last Sunday.

blue was his much favorite
so I thought of wearing something…
'something that can't be seen
only the true candid skin will speak.'

waves more demanding than the past
when the dark lacy blue became more perpendicular.
as you switch off, a weekend
turns with a different glare only to find
how hopelessly you have burnt your hands
along with the rest.

some type and skype
only a shameless gallop out from
a stubborn old friend who turns
a gigolo, after twenty eight years…

nothing truer, nothing more virtual…

the window seller

(ii)

over the bridge
the southern sky redden
to meet the barge that just
harbored. the rift was busy.
I lay down my cup on the bedside
table and saw the border in the
horizon tinge with a longing to
come back.

tell me the new exchange value
please can I hold you a while
let your lids droop down the punctuations
lips of fragrance, damn those encounters
where poppy fields lay awake to wait a
thousand miles

it's a sailing day tomorrow
between Mars and the Indian Ocean
my cup stands beyond, furthermore
than I imagine to forget Harare or
Mozambique

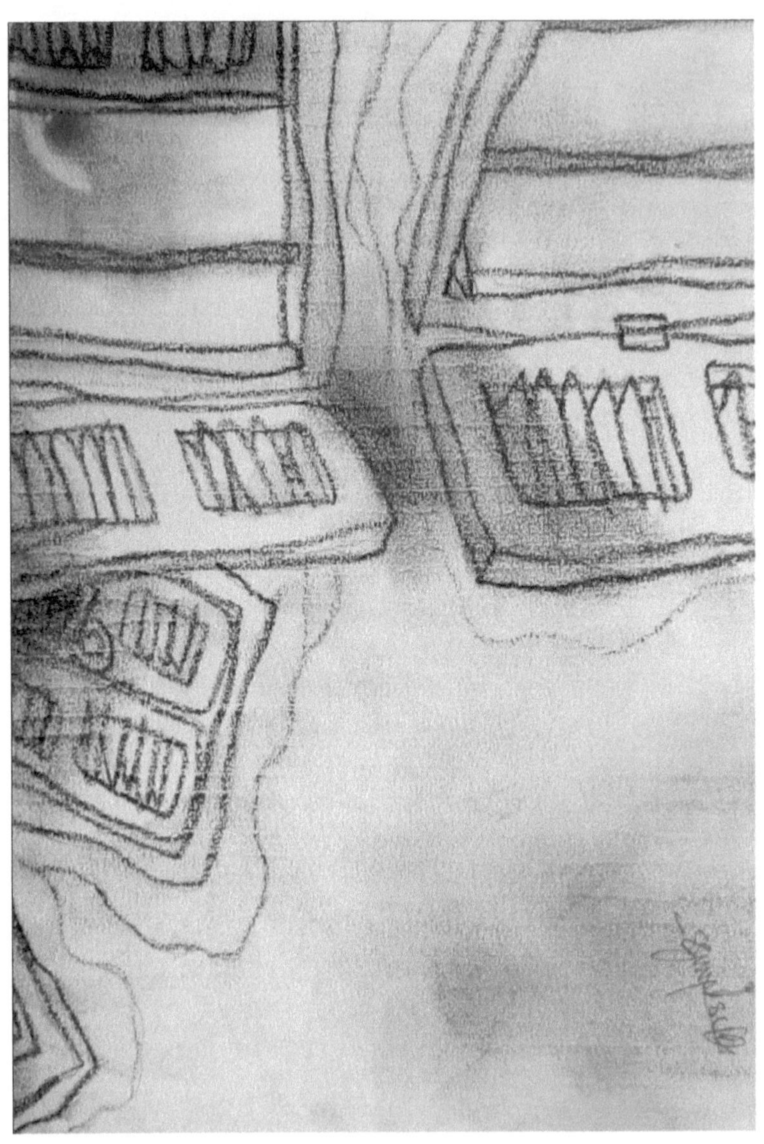

the window seller

(iii)

after miles of unspoken synonyms
as you touched me on my forehead
drenched it with a cologne of gloom
music and mirth, a bell rang away
secret hills and forests and oops!
breezing by colors of a pine evening
just below the aurora borealis
I opened my windows.
grid and hinge, by palm and lips
smelled your palette while a desperateness
shadowed, through the Columbus-route
a land surrounded by water
where my crimson frock entwined thousands
of blue positrons.

so, nothing between us
just a last page left for the pomegranate
woods: "won't you draw a world for me,
my window-seller?"

the brothers

the staircase tinged with blue
glass designed to be a mirror.
a face unlit by a match
opened the narrow door to a
large big window-pane whose
one axis was mine, the other
entirely yours.

three coffee mugs confined to
wear a soft delinquent evening
stared at me in surprise,
"why dear? can't you recognize
the brothers?"

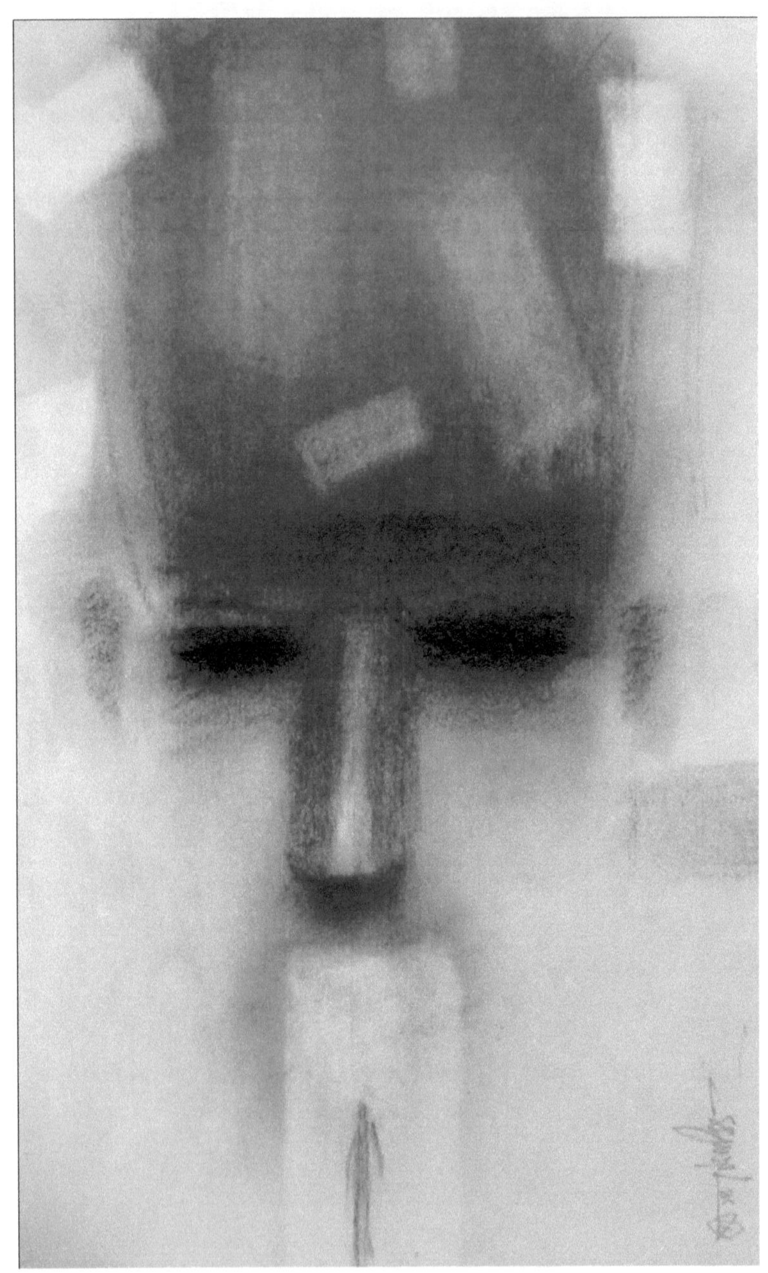

murshidabad

fodder branches
lay still on high stacks
ripe yellow hay crisped away
the husks for the cow and calf

just another morning at the
harvest room, icicled doors bewitched
by the teeth of tide, vacant dusts
as the river Bhagirathi *flows quietly*
along the nawab's diwani-i-aam
the hazar-duari, or the thousand doored
palace vows to glance at each other
door-by-door.

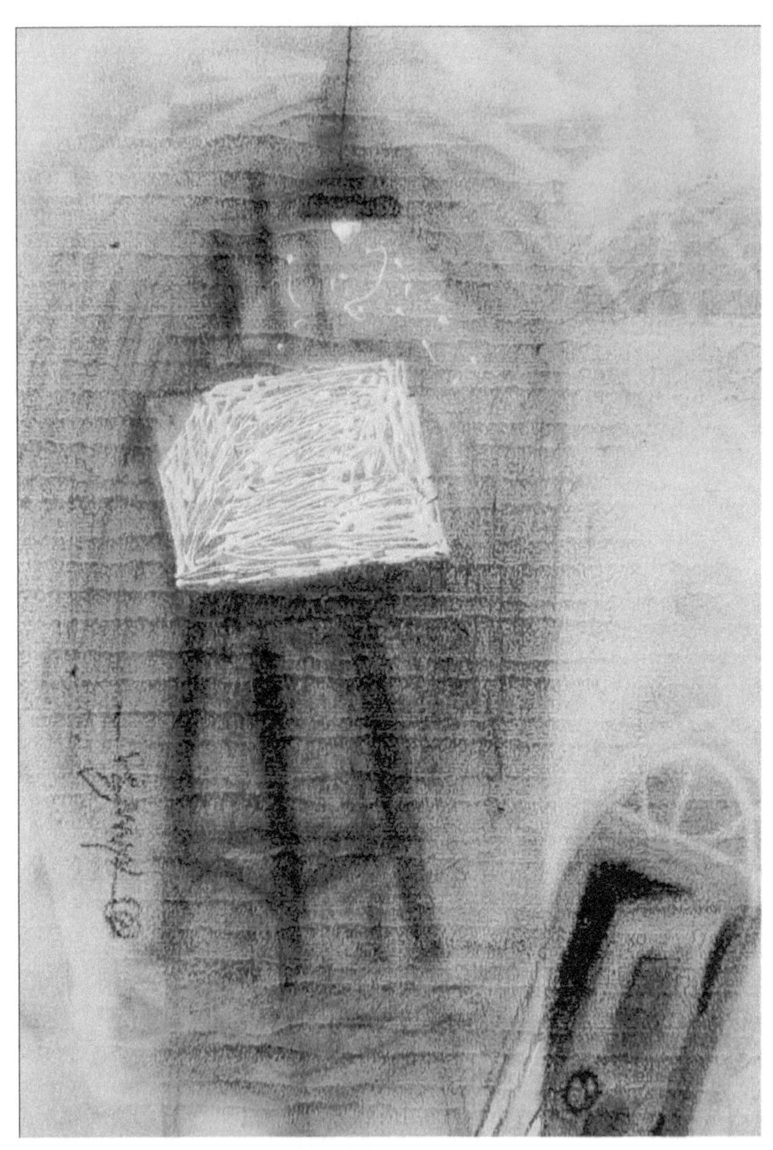

the solitary artist

diffuse a twilight ray
mix water, sienna, salt with burnt amber
a wink of your eye sprinkles the earth
with fire. eroding sands that lay
ahead of time, its dusk, when you play, win
or lose.

the evening gets bribed
shoe-laces don't bother
tears once swallowed
laden with rain colors unfurl deep strokes.
angry cotton fur are left aloof
over a dry brown Bregenz *villa. much later*
as the light crosses the sea, it's a e-link
sent to the boatman via farewell.

last night
a trail of windows caught fire
the whole village died, leaving
no one to decipher the conversation.

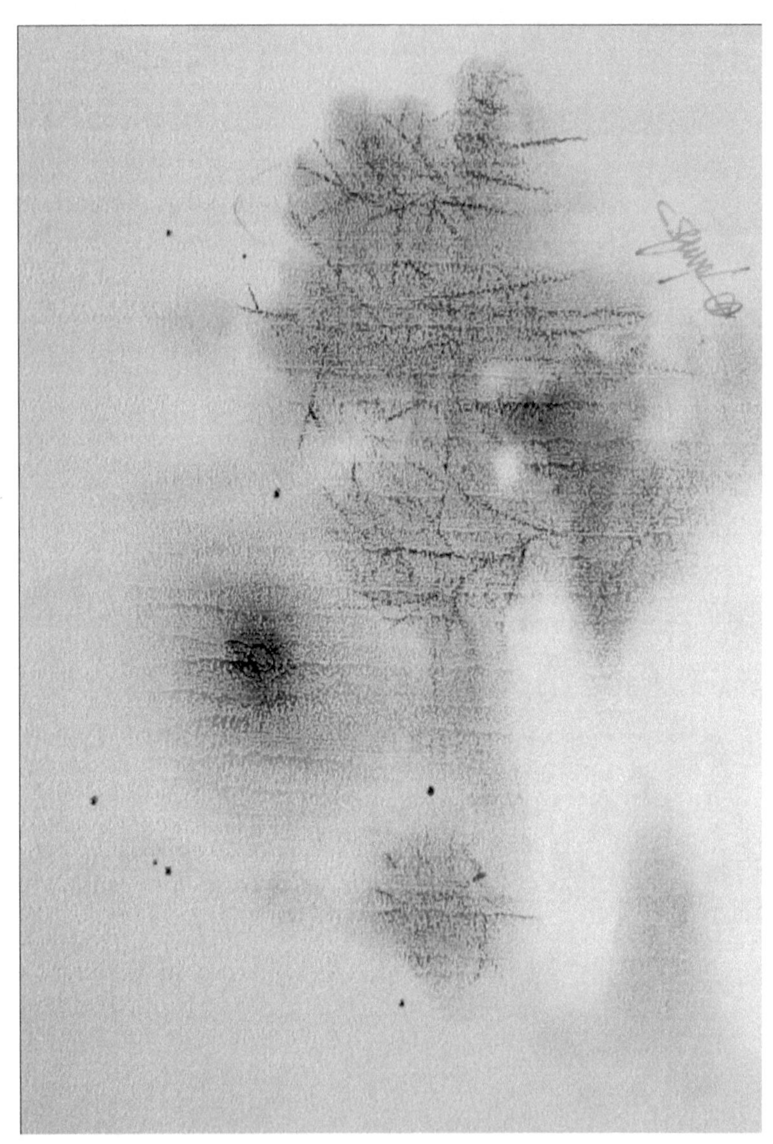

Igls: a thirsty village

this is Igls, sweetheart, where we met by a crystal stream
where silence crosses its fingers to bend down a foot-bridge
beware of oaths, staunch promises, undercurrents of long friendships
broken and slumbering windows, still so stingy. a little bushy village
a drizzle with the Alps clouding closer to you and me.

my hands wet with holding an umbrella
while we missed the last train coming back
wooing down a red hood of a chapel, a clock struck three
to sit back quietly as to pass the flag of silence
blooming between us

no oblivion can break open, hence…

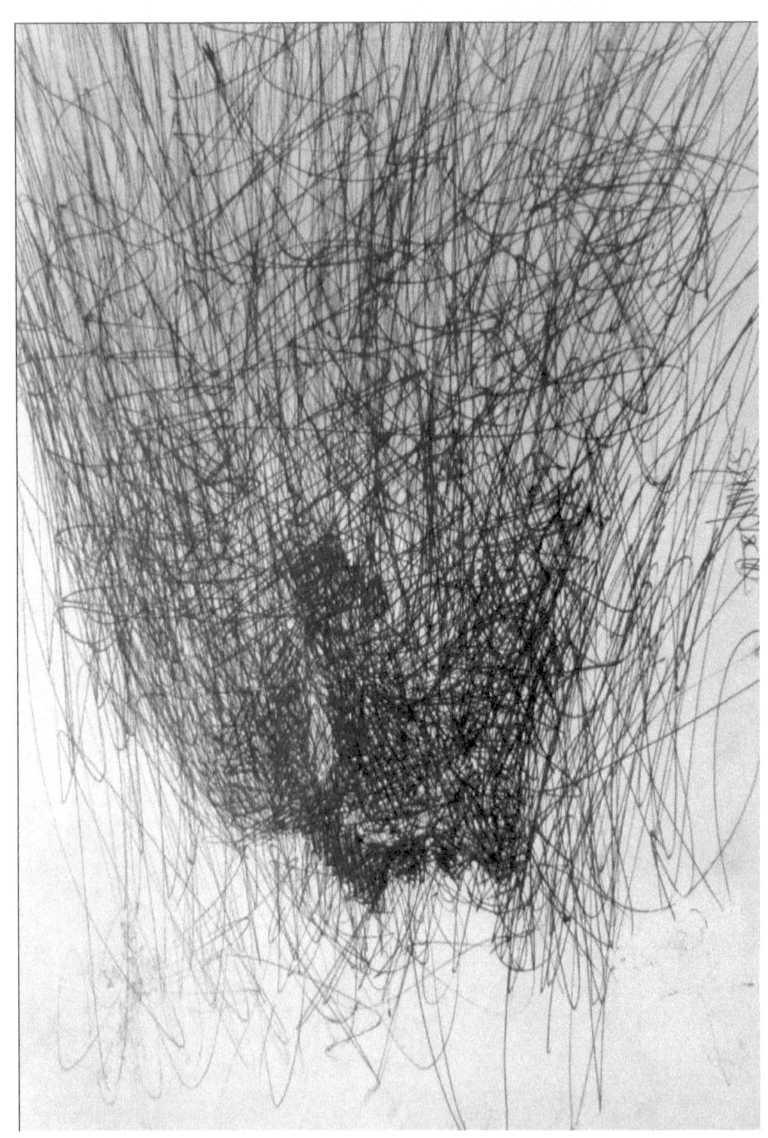

no

starting windows as I pack my things
for a lone station. "are you really going?" chirping orange
leaves cuddled a squeak of a squirrel photographer
warmth centered round my face, feet felt an old caress
a froth blued and brimmed over a spectacle
to tear me in- between. "did I wrong you somewhere?"
a golden wing gushed past years to flow
sweeping across delta rooms which were my shelter

open a folder
map down a new page
lips cursing each other in a vehement 'no.'
drowning day after day, I move out a little window
stuff the letters behind

no more carry- forwards, please…

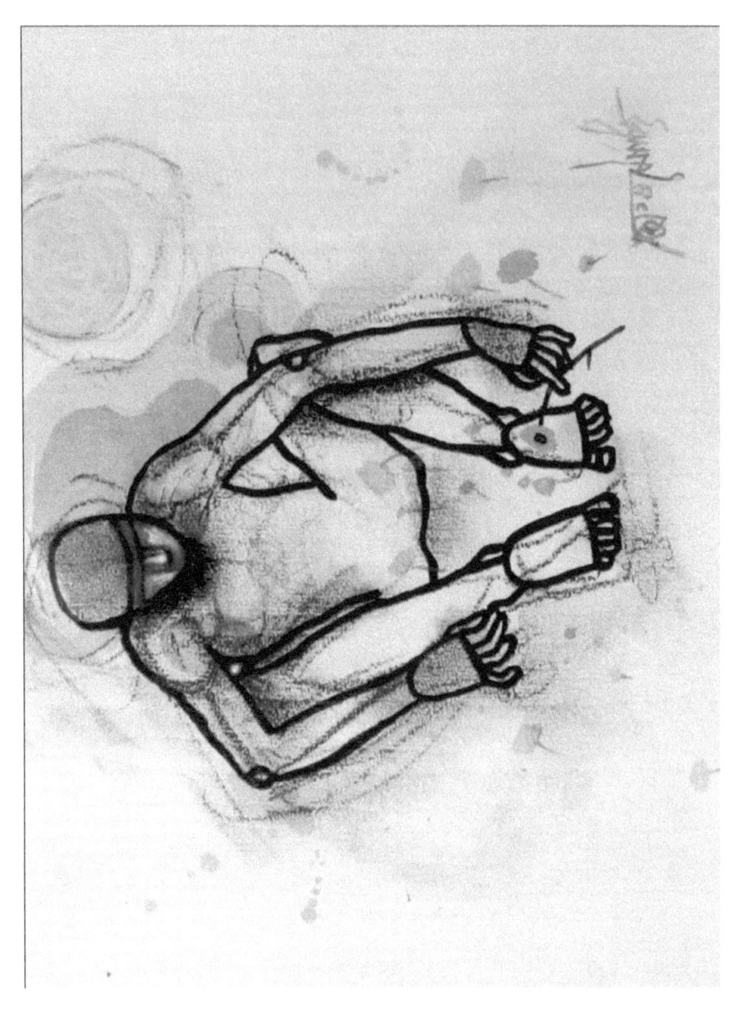

tears on the Danube

I knew your shreds and shadow;
I knew you had a new phone number.
awaiting long hours beside a juniper
I saw the evening lavender buds
about to prosper. the wind knew the rest.

the winter chirped its way down the
Danube gates. I shout for your chest
the apple orchard, the seedling threads
as you painted and writhed with pain
the Danube listened while I closed my eyes
from you, the hills were pouring old leaves
to scatter the evening in uneven drops of rain.

would you mind borrowing a tear
would you mind slaying the mere
images, those that burnt the night in the fire place
above all fears, customs or a lovely shower?

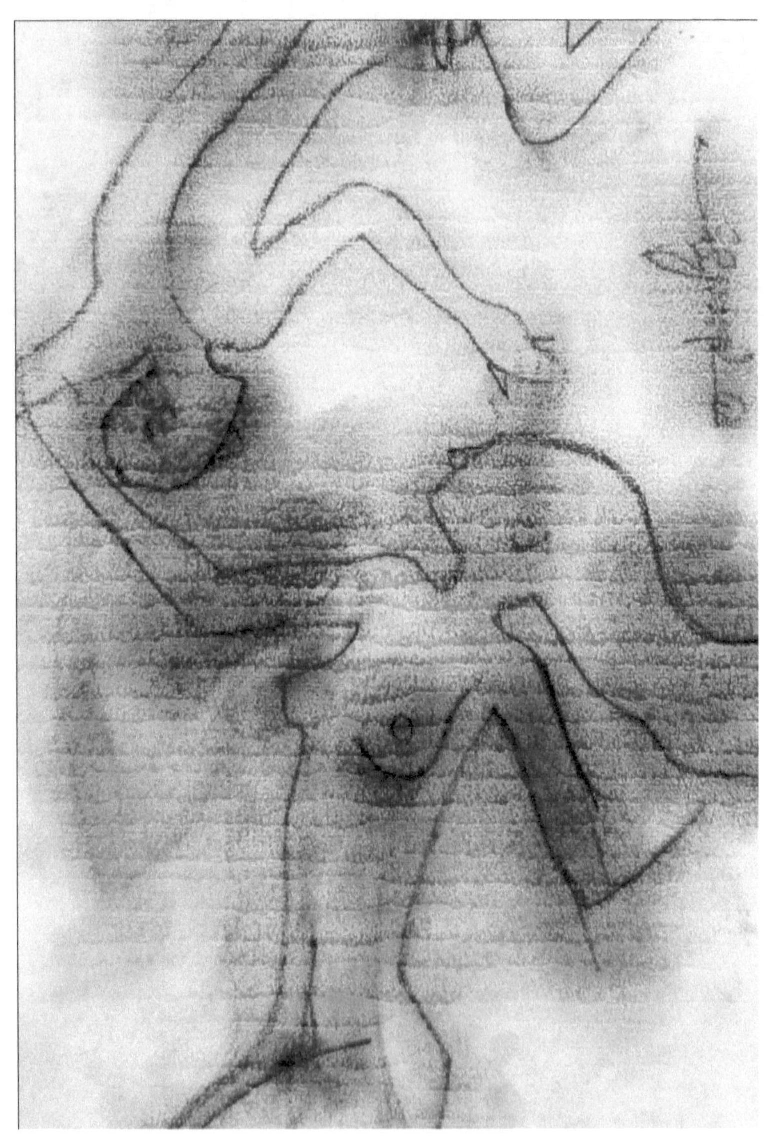

the native

the phenomena of unpacking
tiffin-cases, cardigans, or soaked
plastics stuffed with canned tentacles
cold milk odor merged with definite
beer beverages, when I felt all the corks missing.

the caravan-puller was obscure
nor the galaxy or the savage star-groups
starting off by now to another voyage.
opening to a new verb order
simple bruises of arithmetic, to wait beside
a platform, a mega bus-stop
where compensatory sleep deficits were
challenged as the setting sun rays
trickled the venetian blinds

tried to be another SIM identity
my last name, only to find
you have already left
the precious afternoon

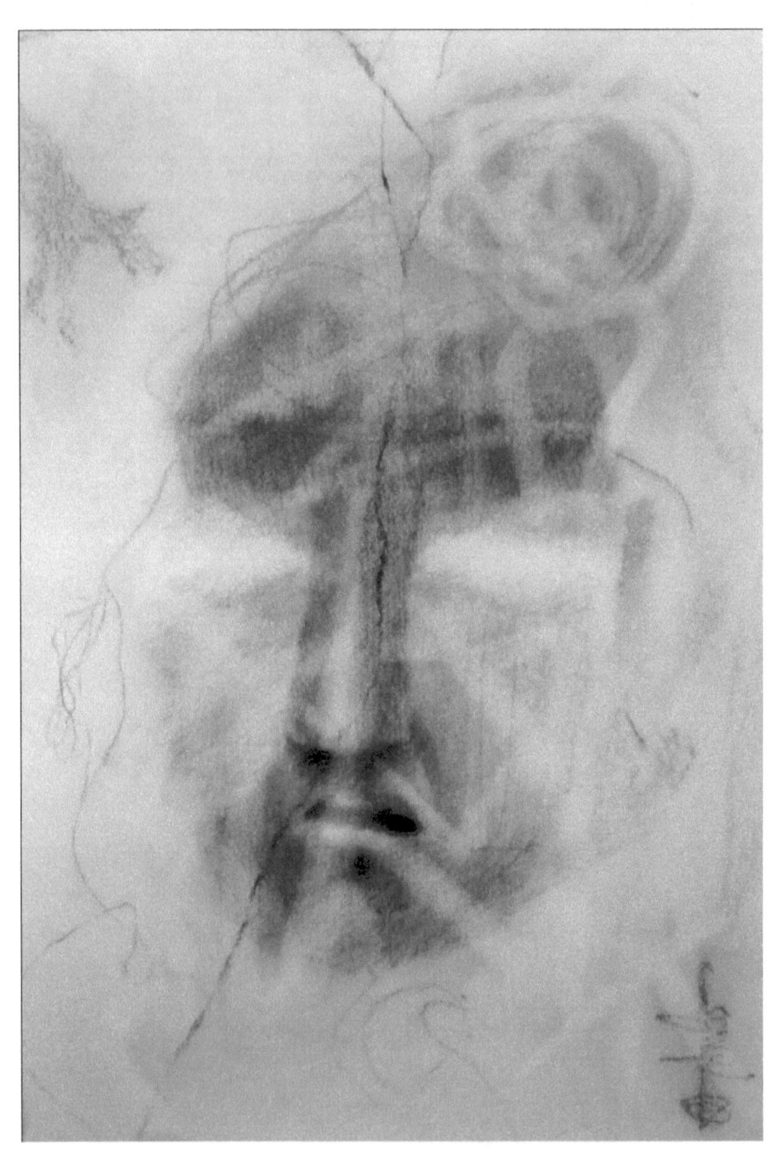

stitching time

silences
closed both ways by brackets
afternoon yarns of wool tangled
on mum's wrists and knees

harrowed cries of puppies along
cold nights of snow and rain
I miffed a frown and slept aside

pattering of the grey verandah
the barren slope bushed with fudges
of unpaired hoofs when the shutter
had to be closed finally

a silence of fog
dewed with spectacles hazy
where the night overspills its tears
scars of open lines without paragraphs
tear out your sophomore siblings

the gruel I borrowed
standing for two hours in a line
had silences yet to be told.

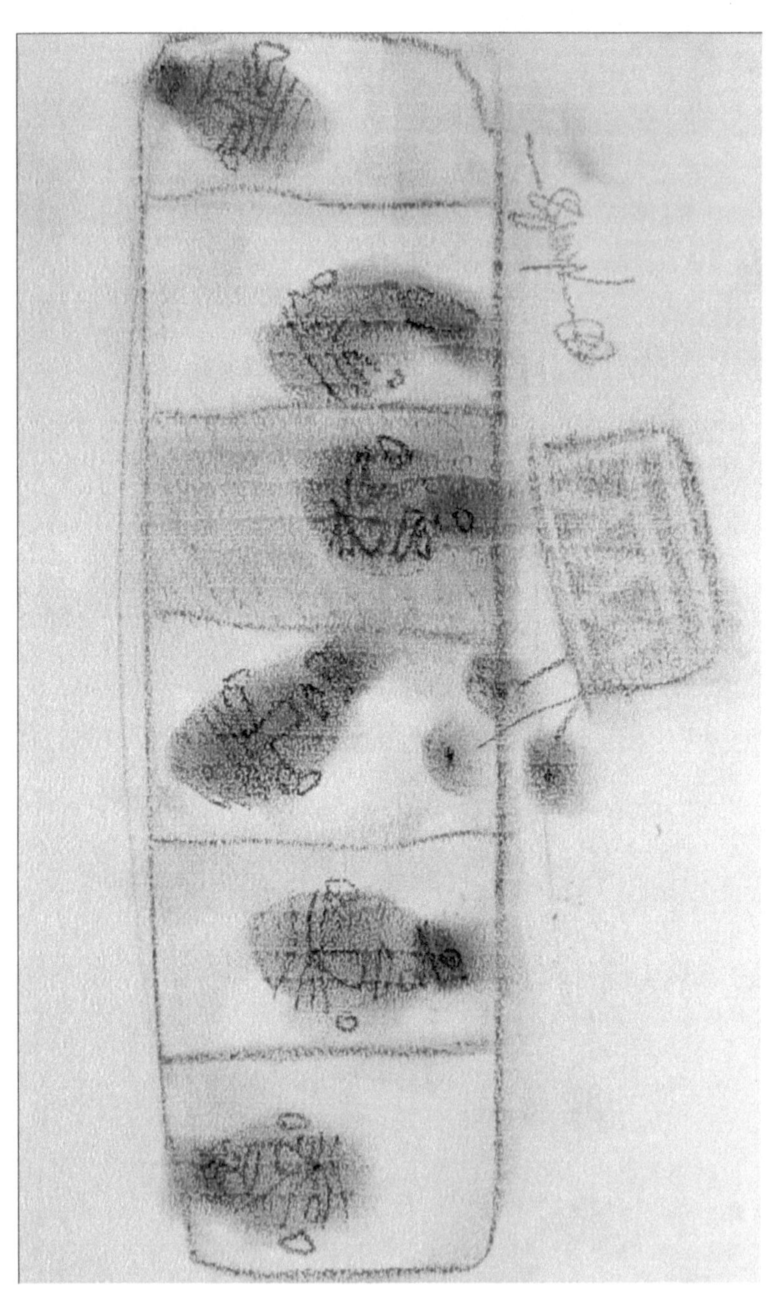

ash Wednesday

in front of the open eyed camera
like a golden oriole dipping down
a sea-storm I gushed into sand dunes
only to lose my breath for the hundredth of time
when the evening waters receded dreadfully
clouds of pain juxtaposed with glee and rainbows
merged into a dominion of the streets of Paris
women engulfing men in a move so sudden
that the petals of the birch, fruits of horse chestnut
tend to tumble over the snow, chrysanthemums
come so near that they feel free to embrace
an ash Wednesday.

a small corner of this pub laughs at your delay
footsteps, open garages, balconies strike out your roll
mark you absent and you, a forlorn hero
bask your way through the Queen's Lane
where, emerged in a large canvas
dip your forehead into the colors
mixed with a deep enchantment, smell of lilac
and etcetera…

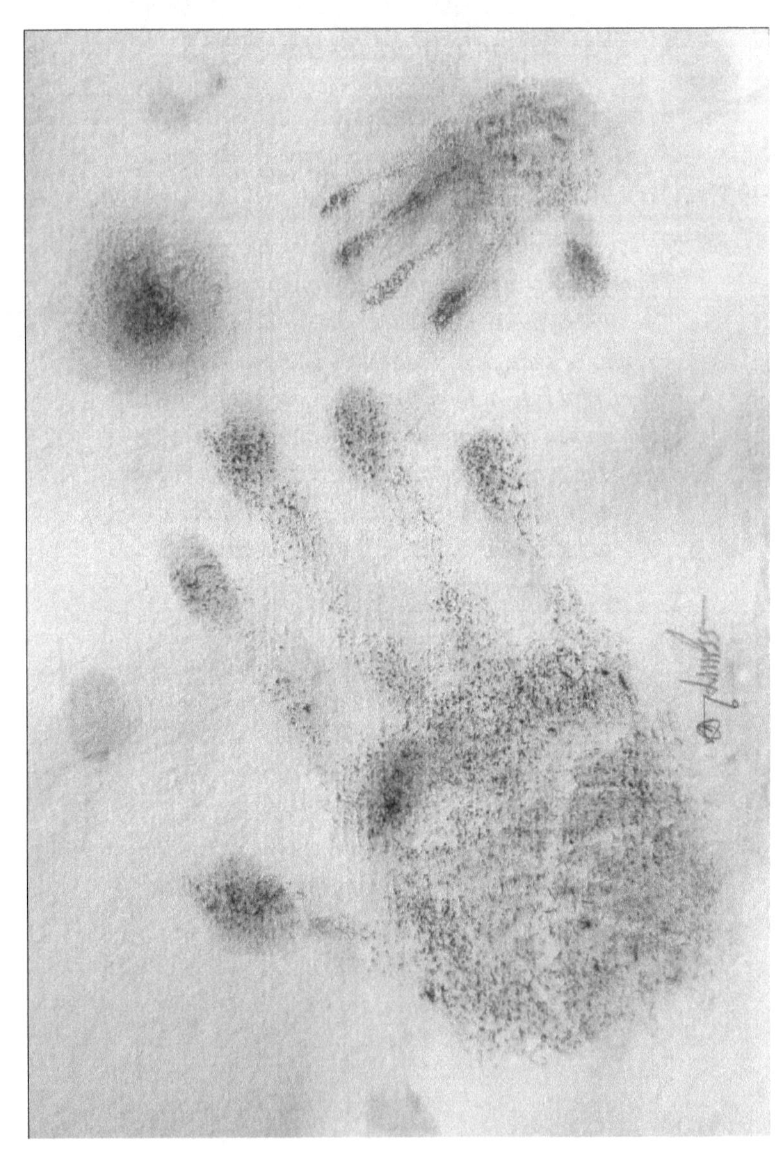

the red planet

brittle pockets
ringing shillings to turn into a new leaf
the street café near the lake-side tavern
a will to sit a longer way
the voice turned hoarse, rang a sad note
a Mahler symphony clung me to my long coat
I forgot my color, the shoes, the stripes
on the zebra path that I had crossed for years

nothing shall I say
to cross the borders of my gender
my inheritance, a gold dangler
a chest of old letters whose ink has slumbered

you know my core is hotter
but you, my ultimate one
would you paint me blue instead?
I too need a shelter
four walls of my own, a kid,
and a fireplace.

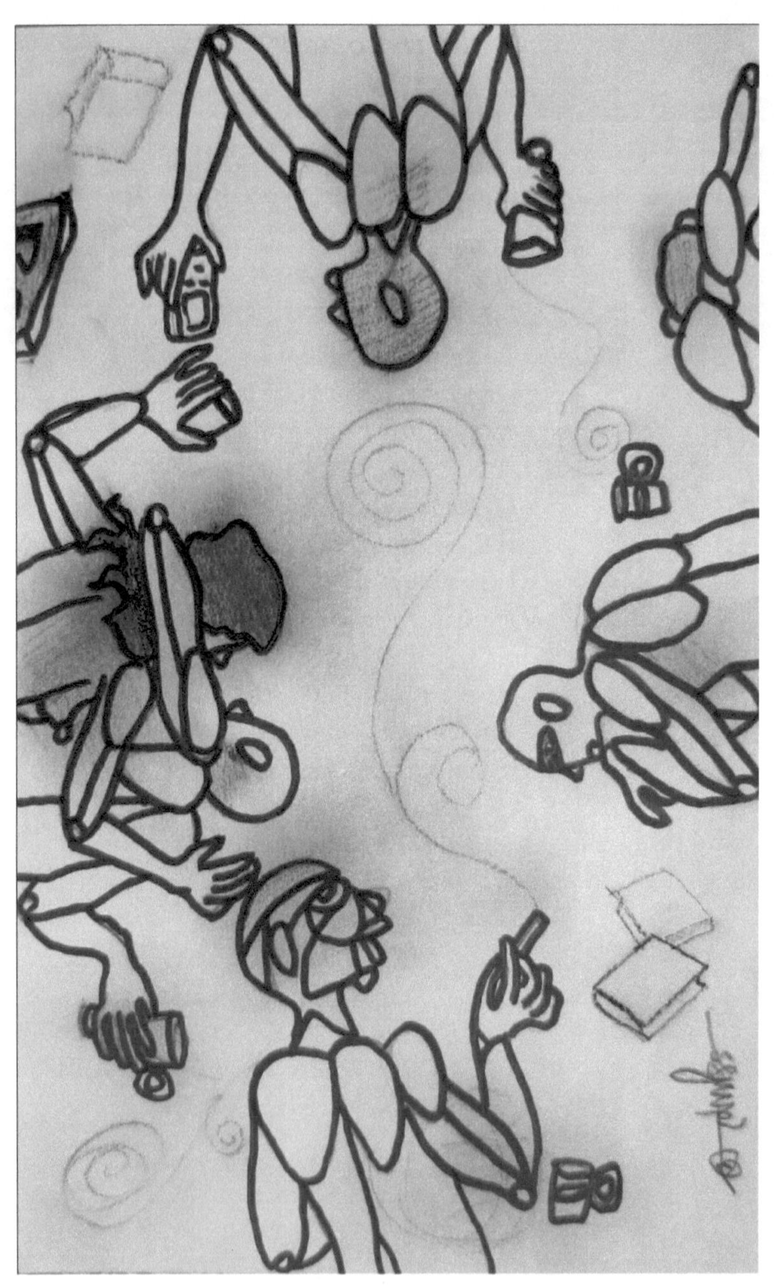

little Oxford

the blueberry muffin
smudges between lips and butter
sky away with penguins that Sandra
dreamed of, the perched honeycombed
dresses of a peculiar leaf shades the band
a man tunes the morning, soothes it and
breaks into loud chorus with Indian leather bags

this is the purple Oxford corner
below the maple, by a roadside pub
come down, my man
brew me a cuppa, the last gulp of the wind
and I fly away this very night
via Emirates.

together

a land over the wide blue Nile
the night changeth yielding place
to morning hue, no borders known
by which you may arrive at G.M.T.
the zero moment of shades, light and dark
under the white foamy cumulus canopy
dense clouds over blue streaks, the northern sky
blushes away from a lost friend.
I await his footsteps. windowpanes clutter
the mirror vibrates the house inside.
it's dinner hour already. honey, open your skype
see who is sitting in front of you, blow out
the last candle, break open the chord
cut the cake, dear, happy birthday!

an age behind

only water
overwhelmed through tears
the road beside Dean Court Avenue
nearing the Matthew Arnold School
looks up the window where a lady
pops out her whole wheat head
a drizzle lets her down with the horizon

miles away my previous births
I came to know right at the moment
how forgotten memories have been
unwound like silk, like wool in an
old woman's afternoons

I came to know my lost mother
a great linguist diving deep towards
the Saraswati river through Rig-vedas,
in a brilliant blue saree
engulfing the line of the equator.

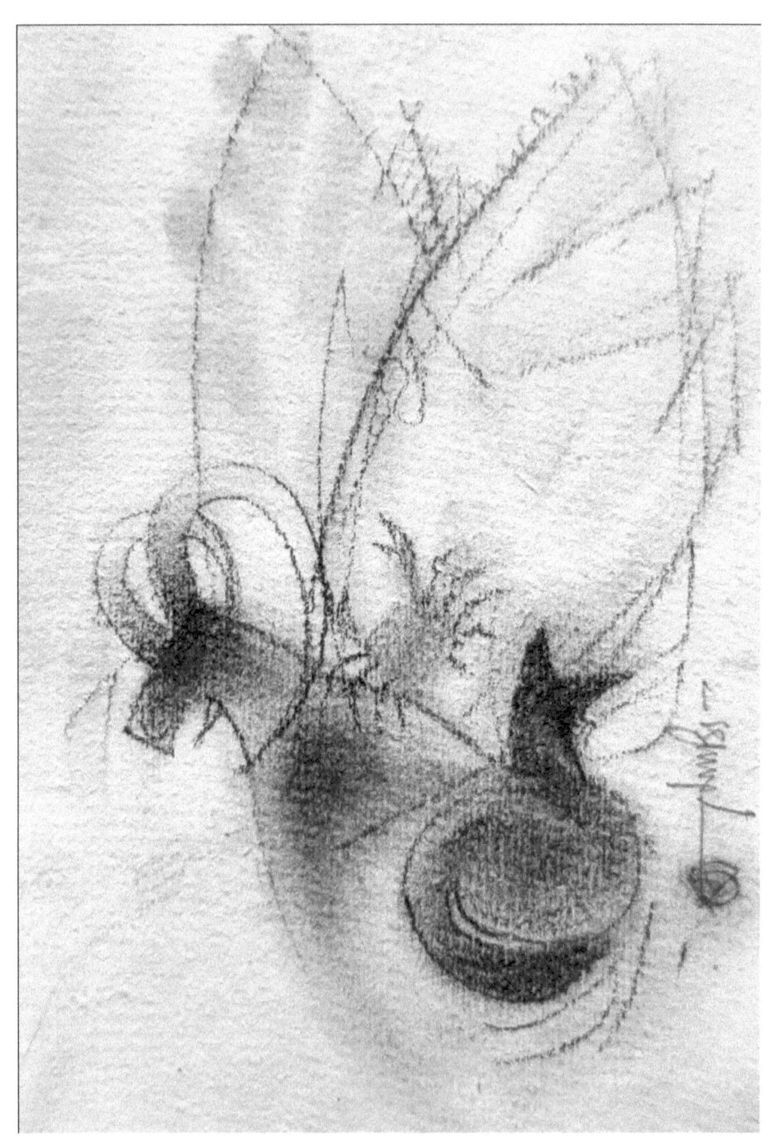

the black and the red

look behind the open horizon
she, the penumbra point lies down
on the road and the pinning oxygen drops
the birds gushed down over and beyond;
where tomorrow ends its sorrow-line, magic
where today emerges the bright red head
with all fingers crossed, look out for a desolate
blue, eight thousand feet above the sea.

open the hair-band
let the evening flow down in struggling
cascades, let me come in, my love—
I, the lonely crimson streak that bands
your hair of darkness, dear lady…

engulf this side of the earth
signal the moon and stars
the Capricorn girl struggles to fly off
and a punch of the colored palette
suddenly oozes all the read purple yellow
reading and blinding my last gaze.

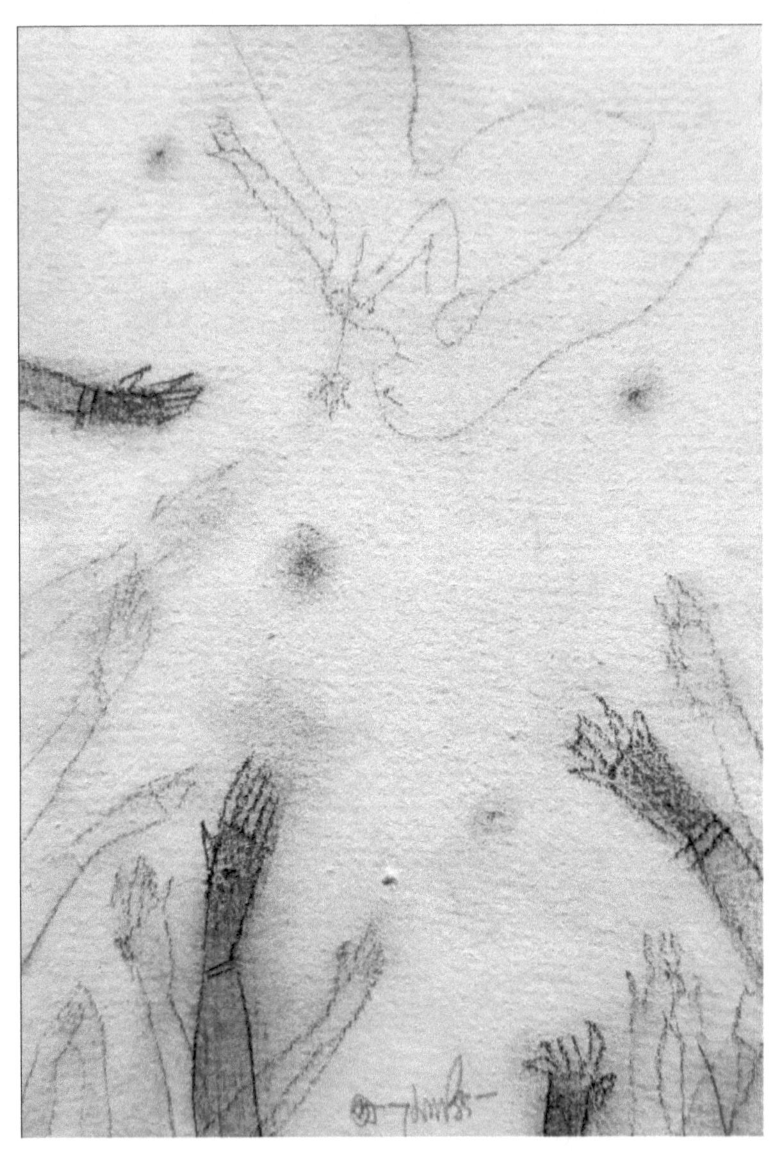

the morning star

words hidden inside
the womb of a black slumbered girl
shriveled strings of hair contaminated
a sonorous secrecy prevails

still the morning comes
droplets tinge the ocean of gods
the cancer, the Capricorn removes
a last lump of a dirty flesh along the night
doors are crossed with huge glaciers
the sea only moves its wings
her feet remain dumb for years

I come by your side sleepy-head
orange your face with vermillion
sleep encompassing all reception of
touch, I allow myself to over-pour tears
and lo! It's a new reddening, forehead
turns the morning leaf to run afar

a land where no girl ever had dared
seed into a man.

snaps

a stray book corner at this side of the street
overflowed music and tingles brewing in
four cups of coffee, though we are all hungry.
just the next door beside the Trinity College
they make bacon sandwiches, mint and parsley
lemons sprinkled over a green-white moon
ponytailed by red and yellow bell peppers. Add on
broccoli and mushrooms, if you please.

a bell rings the chapel tower
three in the afternoon when I overlooked
a dark cloud arising out of nothing
to claim an alien to me I gulped down
the frothy caffe-latte

as I climb up the hill the clouds said,
"hi," and suddenly I realized there was
a rainbow over the southern sky!

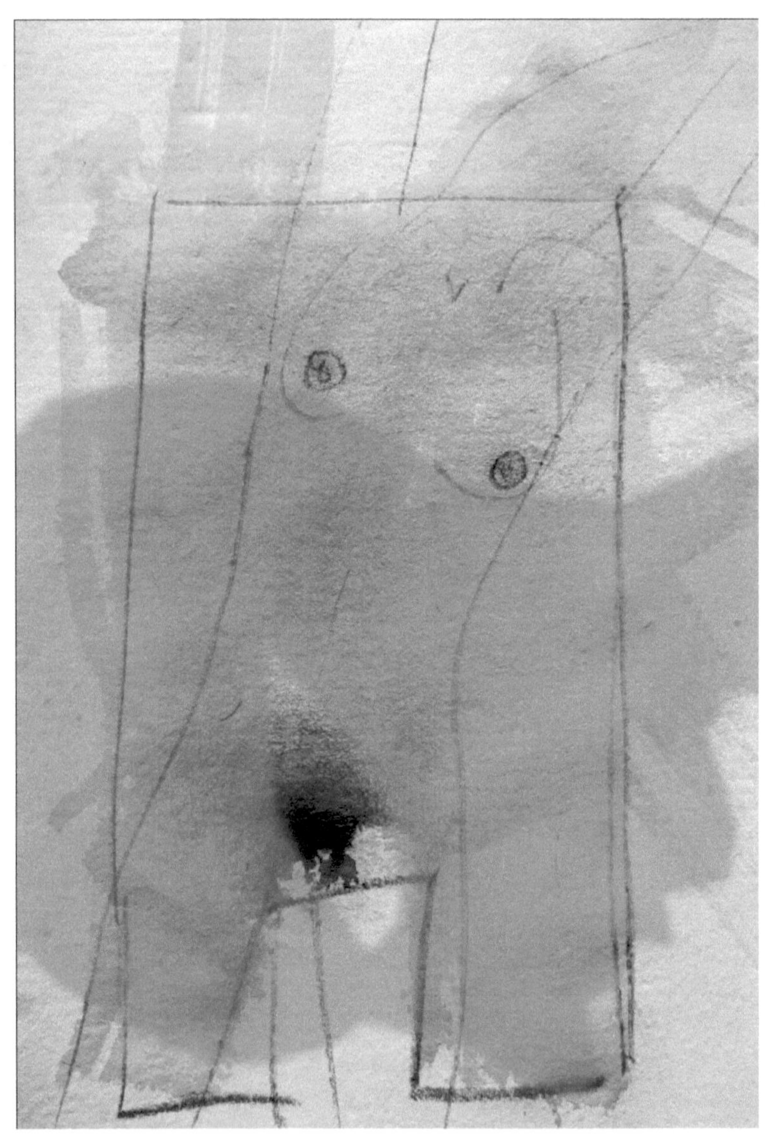

madness

heart of hearts
towards an ugly tunnel
a blind energy emanating
suddenly the truth entered the door
"heathen! you are a liar!"
me? a gasp subdued its tongue
ruling fingers tried to submerge
my past. end chat history. erase.
open in a separate file and delete older

the sturdiest ugliest tunnel
roaded towards an enormous aura
of light, no, not light, may be an open-tide
or, as I struggled to tear open my eyes
Lord, it is a waterfall, the cry where music
can lead us only through mystic paths
not a single ferry can lower so down a depth
to gasp a truth and feel the
mad in you!

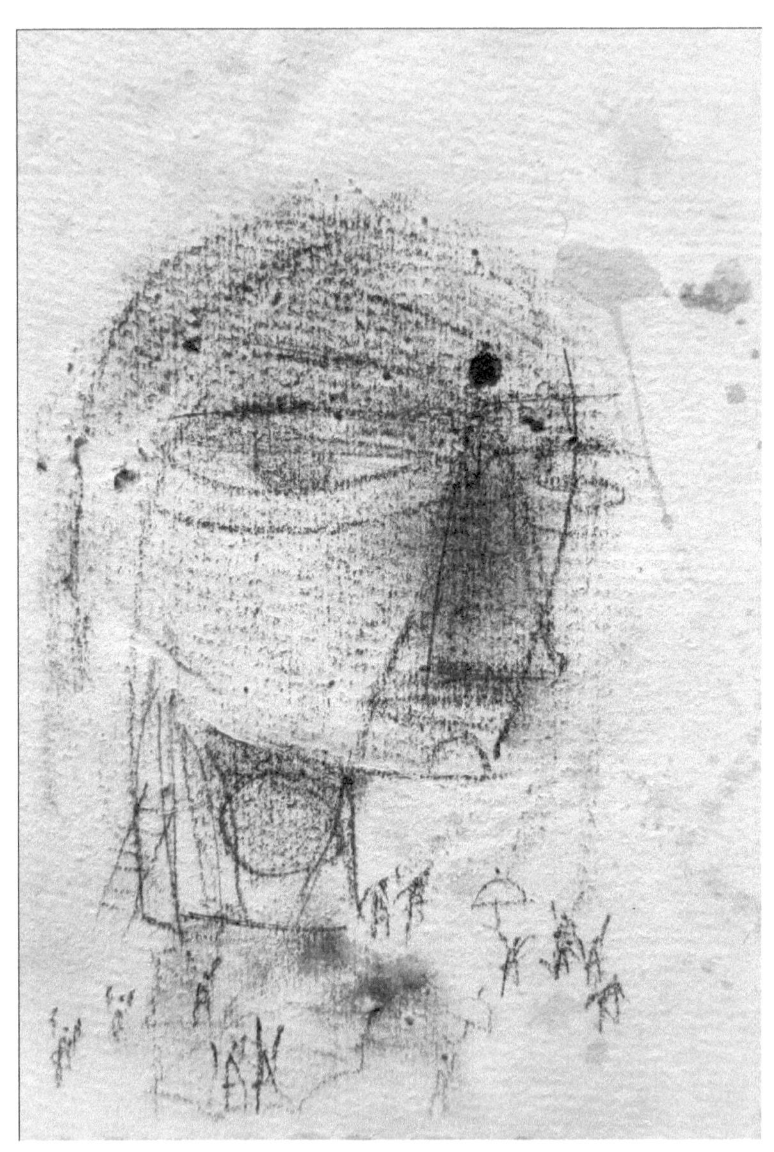

symphony

the shreds of unconscious
thirst
the terminal point of trauma, prior to
this birth or the one ahead

the letter unforgiving, which suffered
from a fear of losing you. am I a
beggar that I owe you my death
allowances, or the memories of the
last number!

Mahler popped in for a break
a wave of hand and the sun-kissed
flamingoes set off to the unknown.

the 'hello' window

last month we saw each other
last month amidst lengthy chapters
with formal beginnings and formal ends
good morning and good night could be spelled

a year passed by
none of us spelled those words correctly.
blue mascara with a brown lip-color
sat beside each other with their backs
a glowworm at last tried to utter a voice.

last week the window opened.
I awaited with beating heart inside the
g-talk machine where modern times had
carved an evening out of nothing.

it was on an offer that I had to
sell off my ink, scribble network
messenger and whatsapp. I blocked myself
to others.

brooding

looked up to see the mast fade away
the classroom swerved a cry
it was a traffic signaler waving
his hands overhead, where the bridge meets
a taxi-driver, my savior,
who opens a wide space and leaves me
to condense my tears, elongate and burst down.

open the dry sherry
put my instauration in half shot glasses
drink life to itself. "cheers!" now I was
riding another bridge by open proportions
that we call smile, frolic and fun.

brood on a cup of tea
mask your face with leaves
red and wild.

the story of three mugs

I know I've wronged you
so much so
the sky between us—
the violets
a bunch of rhododendrons
withered away in silence…

going through the way to
the Trinca's once again
after many light years...
a voice inside bloomed up
I felt, three rejected cups
warm with a cozy welcome
smile awaiting a window shower
drenched to the skin…

I felt
I should say,
"thank you, my dear friend."

Postscript

I think a painting speaks in multiple ways. It loves to talk to the spectators; loves to mingle with them. A painting or a photograph is not confined within its measurement, it depicts a story — a story that revolves around some moments! *The Window Seller* tells a story that does not exclusively belong to the artist, but this is a story of the solitude, which is shared by any creative individual. This does not manifest in all, I believe, the expression is often recessive — confined within the silent soul. This is commonly shapeless. A window denotes some achievements, losses, even some memories of joy and gloom. Again, a window gives passage to fresh air into the conscious as well as the subconscious minds. I am much elated that my paintings received their completeness with the poems of my favorite poet Ballari Sen. She has colored my effort and has given wings to my dreams that will now traverse to the infinite. This book and its source are undoubtedly the expressions of my *Prana.* I dwell in them.

Thank you so much, Ballari.

Tamojit Bhattacharya
28th April, 2014
12 No. Chalklane, Uttarpara, Hooghly,
West Bengal, India - 712258
Email: 7sokal@gmail.com

About The Author

Ballari Sen (Ph. D.) is the Assistant Professor, Department of Bengali, Gokhale Memorial Girls' College, Calcutta. She is an award winning poet (she received the much coveted *Krittibas Puraskar*) for her Bengali poetry book, *Bihaan Raater Bandish. The Window Seller* is her maiden venture in English-language poetry. She is now doing her post-doctoral research work with Prof. Aditi Lahiri, and Dr. Stephen Parkinson on the interface of Portuguese and Bengali in middle Bengali texts at the University of Oxford. She can be reached on: ankhiballari@gmail.com

www.ingramcontent.com/pod-product-compliance
Lightning Source LLC
LaVergne TN
LVHW041755190726
843493LV00008B/2637

* 9 7 8 9 3 8 3 8 8 8 1 4 6 *